Fire HD 8 Manual User Guide

Manual for Fire HD 8

By Emery H. Maxwell

Table of Contents

Welcome

Welcome to the *Fire HD 8 Manual User Guide*. This manual is intended to help you understand and manage the different features of the *Kindle Fire* tablets, focusing primarily on the *Fire HD 8* device.

Starting with the basics, this book is intended to help you understand what the *Kindle HD 8* device can do and how to do it.

Using the *Fire HD* tablet might be simple, but not everything about it is entirely intuitive. In fact, trying to figure it out by yourself can be overwhelming, especially if you have never owned a tablet before.

This is where a guide can be very useful.

This guide is intended to help improve your understanding and usage of the *Kindle HD Fire* tablet, including how to maximize it's features.

It will cover:

How to set up the *Fire HD 8*

How to Navigate *Fire HD 8*

• How to download content

• How to install and delete apps

• How to set up a keyboard

• How to connect the tablet to a printer

• How to set up and access email

• How to customize the settings

• How to take pictures, share photos, and transfer them to a computer

• How to use the Micro-SD card

• How to use the voice command feature

Troubleshooting

• . . . and more.

It's time to get started.

Getting Started

The following chapters will help you understand the *Kindle HD 8* device. They will go over specifications, button navigation, status indicators, and setting up *Kindle HD 8*.

Specifications

In the Box: *Fire HD 8* tablet, USB 2.0 cable, 5W power adapter, and Quick Start Guide

Display: 8" HD

Resolution: 1280 x 800

Weight: 13oz

Dimensions: 8.4" x 5.0" x 0.4"

Generation: 7th generation – 2017 release

Processor: Quad-core 1.3 GHZ

Connectivity: Dual-band a/b/g/n WI-FI

Audio: DOLBY ATMOS, dual stereo speakers, built-in microphone, 3.5mm stereo jack.

Storage: 16 or 32GB, but can be expanded by as much as 256 GB

Battery Life: Up to 12 hours (will vary based on device settings, usage, web browsing, and downloading content.

Charge Time: Fully charges in under 6 hours using the micro-USB power adapter included in the box.

Sensors: ACCELEROMETER, ambient light sensor

Ports: USB 2.0 (micro-B connector) to connect to a PC/Macintosh computer, or to charge the device with the included power adapter; MICROSD slot for external storage

CPU & RAM: Quad-Core 1.3 GHZ, with 1.5 GB of RAM

Location Services: Location-based services via WI-FI

Camera Specs: VGA Front-facing Camera. 2.0 MP rear-facing HD camera

Cover: Sold separately

ALEXA Enabled: Yes, press and ask

Exterior Buttons (Basic Hardware)

T o switch on the tablet, press and hold the power button for a few moments. It is located at the top-right corner of the device.

The Micro-SD slot, which can be used to expand the device's memory, is also located toward the top, and to access it, the small hatch must be opened. Once opened, the Micro-SD memory card can be connected.

The volume buttons are located on the left side of the device.

The microphone is located at the center.

The charging port is located next to the microphone.

The stereo jack input is located further down, toward the top-left of the device. This is where headphones can be inserted.

When you see six small gaps lined up in a row, that is the speaker.

When you want to turn off the device, simply press and hold the power button until an icon emerges, prompting you to confirm the shutdown process. It should read: *OK* or *cancel.*

Setting Up The Kindle Fire

After powering on the *Kindle Fire* tablet for the first time, a series of prompts should pop up. The questions are fairly straight forward, but this guide will walk you through them step-by-step.

First, you must wait for the tablet to load.

Initially, when finished loading, the screen should read: **Welcome**.

You should be allowed to choose your language. Be careful and try not to rush. It can be easy to inadvertently tap the wrong icon. To make things easier, you can select a larger text size by adjusting the icon at the bottom-left portion of the screen.

When you're finished selecting your language of choice, tap *Continue*.

Next, the screen should read:

Connect to a WI-FI Network

Locate and select your network, then tap *Connect* to access it. If this is your first time using the device, you will probably need to enter a password first.

If you do not know your WI-FI password or which network you use, refer to your Internet Service Provider or router manufacturer.

Multiple WI-FI connections can be established. To establish them, pull down the main menu by swiping the top portion of the screen. Then go to the *Wireless* icon. If WI-FI is not switched on already, switch it on. Then tap *Add Network* and type in the name of the network you would like to establish. Then type in the password, and you should be good to go.

Allow several moments or so for it to connect. Once connected, it should begin loading.

It may or may not need to install a software update. If it does download and install an update, it can take at least several minutes or so, and the device may need to be restarted to complete the process.

The next screen should now read:

Register Your Fire

Enter Amazon Account Info

If you don't have an *Amazon* account already, tap the *New to Amazon?* Icon.

Although you can still go web-searching without an account, you will need one in order to download apps, music, books, videos, etc.

At the bottom-right portion of the screen, you can either select *Complete Setup Later* or *Continue*.

If you choose to complete the setup, tap *Continue* and follow the instructions.

If you don't already have your credit card information on file with *Amazon*, you may also be prompted to enter that data. This will make it easier to make purchases through *Kindle* and *Amazon* in general.

When you finish reading through the terms of registration, click *agree* if you agree with them. Then tap the *close* button.

You should now be back at the registration screen.

Tap the *registration* button to complete the registration process.

From there, select a time zone. By default, the device should be able to determine your time zone for you through your network.

After selecting your time zone, click *Continue* at the bottom-right of the screen.

If you have a previous kindle device, perhaps an older one that's already on file, you may be given the option to restore it.

The bottom-right portion of the screen will read: *Do Not Restore* and *Continue*.

If *continue* is selected, follow the prompts on the next screen.

If *Do Not Restore* is selected, it should take you to a screen that reads:

Family Setup

Adult Profiles

Set up Child Profiles?

This is your chance to set up multiple profiles.

If you choose to set up a child profile, read the instructions carefully to avoid being charged after the free trial period.

But if you are an adult and the app is just for you, tap the *Not now* button under **Set up Child Profiles?** Then select *Continue*.

The next screen should read: *No Thanks* and *Enable* at the bottom-right portion. It is asking you if you would like to enable location services.

Enabling location services can make things somewhat easier for certain things online.

To illustrate, if you search for a specific restaurant chain, the website might be able to pinpoint which one of those restaurants is closest to you.

The drawback is that it can use up more battery power, so use it only if you feel like it is necessary.

After that, the next screen should read: **Backup & Auto-Save**

This will help backup your files, pictures, etc, just in case they get lost.

The orange-colored icons on the right side of the screen should each have a dot on the far ride side. This indicates that the files are already saved for you, so this step has basically been taken care of.

Select *Continue* at the bottom-right portion of the screen.

The next screen should read: **Connect Social Networks**

If you do not want to connect to social networks at this time, tap *Continue*.

The next page will go over their coverage plan.

This is where you need to think about how likely or unlikely it is that your device may be damaged.

For example, a person who has young children, dogs, or generally has a history of having their property damaged may want to consider purchasing insurance.

A person who has had little or no trouble with accidental spills, breakages, etc in the recent past may choose to decline.

If you choose to decline, simply select *No thanks, continue without protection.*

The next page should read: **Welcome!**

Select *Start* to begin the tutorial.

Continue to select *Next* as you scroll through the tutorial.

After the tutorial process is finished, set up should be complete.

Navigation Buttons

O n the front of the device, there are three buttons; a triangle, a circle, and a square. They are electronic icons, so the device must be powered on in order for these buttons to be visible.

If the device is powered on and you still can't see the buttons (icons), or if the buttons disappear, simply swipe the bottom portion of the screen until they appear.

The circle is the *home* button. Tapping the *home* button will take you back to the main (home) screen whenever you want to get out of an app.

The triangle button is the *back* button. If you ever want to go back to a previous web-page, simply tap the *back* button. If you want to go back one step, tap the *back* button once. If you would like to go back three steps, tap the *back* button three times, and so forth. If you continue to tap it consecutively, it can eventually take you all the way back to the main screen (homepage).

The square-shaped icon is the *most recent apps* button. This can be useful when you want to return to an app that you were recently using. It will show you all the apps that are currently running.

Having many apps running in the background at the same time can use up more battery power, so you may not want to have many apps running all at once.

To close out the apps that you are not currently using, simply swipe them away until they are no longer on the screen. This will close them.

Status Indicators

The status indicators are located at the top of the main screen (Home screen). They are there to keep you informed of battery status, and activity status. There is a parental controls indicator if you choose to enable it.

If you are reading a book or document, the indicators can still be viewed by tapping the top of the screen. The TOOLBARS should be displayed.

The **Battery status indicator** reveals the various stages of the battery as it discharges. It will display a lighting bolt on the battery icon while the *Kindle* device is charging.

Place your *Kindle* device into sleep mode when you are finished using it. This will help conserve battery life. The *Kindle* can be placed in sleep mode by pressing and releasing the power button.

The battery can be recharged by plugging the *Kindle* into a computer through a USB cable.

The device can also be plugged into a power outlet, although a compatible power adapter will be needed.

While charging, the indicator light on the bottom corner of the device will turn amber. It is important to see this light, so you can confirm that your *Kindle* is actually charging.

When the battery charge is complete, the indicator light will turn green.

The **Activity indicator** can be seen in the top left corner of the *Kindle* screen while it is loading a web page, downloading content, connecting to a network, opening a large PDF file, or checking for new items.

The **Parental Controls indicator** can be seen when Parental Controls are enabled.

Settings Customization

Go to the main page, swipe downward at the top of the screen, and then tap *Settings*.

To change screen's **background (wallpaper)**, go to *Settings*.

1.) Look under the *Device* section

2.) Tap *Display*.

3.) Tap *Wallpaper*

4.) Scroll through the preset list of pictures, then press *Set* after selecting one.

Now when you go back to the homepage, the new wallpaper should be displayed. You can also import custom pictures.

To change the color of the **onscreen keyboard**, go to *Settings*.

1.) Look under *Personal*.

2.) Tap *Keyboard and Language*

3.) Tap *Fire Keyboard*

4.) Tap *Keyboard Color*

5.) Change it from light to dark or dark to light.

By the time you go back to the homepage, the effect should have taken place.

To turn on **keyboard sounds**, go to *Settings*.

1.) Look under *Personal*

2.) Tap *Keyboard and Language*

3.) Tap *Fire Keyboard*

4.) Look to the right of *Keyboard Sounds* and adjust the switch to the *on* position.

To help conserve **battery power**, go to *Settings*.

1.) Look under *Device*

2.) Tap *Power*

3.) Look under *Smart Suspend*

4.) Make sure the switch to the right of *Automatic Smart Suspend* is set to the *on* position.

This will automatically turn off the WI-FI when the tablet is not in use, which will save battery power.

- To **remove adds:**

1.) Go to the *Amazon* website and make sure you are signed in.

2.) Go to *Accounts & Lists.*

3.) Go to *Manage Your Content and Devices.*

4.) Select *Your Devices.*

5.) Look at the actions list. It should show all of your *Kindle* devices.

6.) Click or tap the square box to the left of the device name.

7.) The next window should now include something that reads: *Special Offers / Offers and Ads.* Below that, there should be an *Edit* tab. Tap or click it.

8.) You will have a choice to edit, or in this case, unsubscribe from, the special offers field. But before you click the *unsubscribe* button, take the time to read the warning they give you. They will basically let you know that there is a fee, so make sure you are willing to pay it before selecting *unsubscribe*.

- To **check available storage space:**

1.) Go to *Settings.*

2.) Go to *Storage.* There should be options available to help free up space.

- To **change the name that appears on your device:**

1.) Go to *Settings.*

2.) Go to *Device Options.*

3.) Go to *Change Your Device Name.*

- To **set up multiple profiles:**

1.) Go to *Settings.*

2.) Go to *Registration and Household.*

3.) Go to *Household and Family Library,*

4.) Go to *Add a New Person.*

When creating a new profile, a parental password will need to be set up. This will disallow the other person to access your profile.

- To **lock screen rotation:**

1.) Swipe the top of the screen in a downward motion

2.) Tap *Auto-rotate*

• To **adjust screen brightness:**

1.) Using a downward motion, swipe the top of the screen

2.) Look at *Quick Settings*

3.) Move the slider to lighten or darken the screen.

To **Set a Lock Screen Password or PIN**

Important Note: A lock screen password or PIN can't be turned off if you have *Amazon Free-Time* enabled on your device. This is because it is required to prevent children from accessing adult profiles.

1.) Swipe downward from the upper portion of the screen and tap **Settings**.

2.) Go to **Security**.

3.) Tap the switch next to **Lock Screen Pass-code**.

4.) Tap **PIN** to create a code that consists of at least four numbers. To create a more complex password, tap **Password**.

Apps

The following chapters will deal the apps, including how to locate them, install them, and delete them.

Installed Apps

The apps that are already installed on the tablet (including settings, calendar, clock, internet browser, and email) can be viewed by selecting the *home* tab, and then scrolling down.

The icon, *Silk browser* is basically the internet browser, and it is what you would select when you want to browse the web.

If you scroll back up, you can find an icon titled, *Recent*. It should be located next to the *home* tab. It will show you all of the apps that have been recently running.

Similar to the *most recent apps* icon, it is useful for retrieving apps that had gotten pushed into the background.

If you would like to install an app, such as NETFLIX, go to the *APPS* tab. Then go to the *STORE* tab at the top-right portion of the screen. From there, search for the app you want to download. You can type the name of the app into the search bar. Once the app is found, it can be downloaded.

Any content you download onto the *Kindle* device is automatically saved to the *Cloud*. If your *Kindle* device is ever lost or stolen, your downloads can be downloaded from the *Cloud* onto a different *Kindle* tablet.

How to Delete an App

To delete an app, go to the *APPS* tab. Press and hold the tab of the app you would like to delete until a prompt comes up that reads: *Add to Favorites* and *Remove from Device*.

Tap *Remove from Device*. After a few moments, it should be deleted.

Sometimes, for certain apps, the uninstall process will be somewhat more complex. Sometimes after following the above procedure, it will ask you for confirmation to uninstall it. In this case, tap *OK*, and then it will be deleted.

There are certain apps—such as *Calendar, E-mail,* etc—that come installed with the *Fire* device, and for that reason, they cannot be deleted.

Generally, if you did not download the app, you will not be able to entirely remove it.

Downloading Apps, Games, Music, Books, and Videos

If you want to download music, games, books, videos, or apps, go to the *home* page. From there, scroll through the various icons toward the top of the screen until you find what you are looking for.

The icons should read: *RECENT, HOME, BOOKS, VIDEO, GAMES, SHOP, APPS, MUSIC, AUDIOBOOKS, NEWSSTAND.*

Select the icon you are interested in downloading from. If you want to download a video, select the *video* icon. If you want to download an app, select the *APP* icon.

After selecting an icon, it will take you to another page. You will now need to select the *STORE* icon, which can be found near the top-right portion of the screen.

For example, if you want to download a video, select the *VIDEO* icon, and from there, select *STORE*.

Now you should be able to view the various videos that are available.

The videos that you have already purchased will be available in your library. To access your library, click on the *LIBRARY* tab. It is located next to the *STORE* tab.

In summary, whether you are downloading books, videos, or music, the process is generally the same.

1.) Go to the icon you are interested in downloading from (BOOKS, VIDEOS, AUDIOBOOKS, etc)

2.) Select the *Store* icon.

3.) To view your purchases, go to *Library*

How to Set up a Keyboard

If you have purchased a keyboard to go along with your *Fire*, you can begin setting it up by going to *settings*.

You will need a USB cord, which may or may not have came along with your BLUETOOTH keyboard, to charge it. Make sure it has charged for several hours before you use it for the first time.

From *settings*, go to *Wireless*.

Then select the *BLUETOOTH* tab. Look at the right side of the screen and make sure *BLUETOOTH* is on.

On the keyboard itself, there should be an *OFF/ON* switch. Switch on the keyboard.

Next to the *OFF/ON* switch, there should be a *PAIR* button. Press and hold this button for a few moments.

Now tap words/numbers on the screen under *Available Devices*.

Using your keyboard, enter the four-digit code, then press *Enter*.

Configuration should now be complete.

How to Connect The Tablet to a Printer

As long as your printer supports wireless printing, you should be able to use the printing option from your *Kindle* tablet.

However, not all formats are compatible. Personal documents converted to .AZW (the *Kindle* format) cannot be printed through the *Kindle Personal Documents Service*.

The following formats that are supported are as listed:

• JPEG

• PNG

• PDF

• Microsoft Office files

• WEBPAGES

• TXT

If your printer fails to recognize the *Kindle* tablet, a print plugin can be downloaded from the APP store on your device.

It should also be noted that *Fire* devices do not support the share feature with printing.

To print from the *Kindle* Device:

1.) Power on the printer

2.) Make sure the *Kindle* device and printer are connected to the same internet connection.

3.) Go to the page you want to print

4.) Tap the *Menu* icon (the icon with three dots)

5.) Tap *Print*

6.) When the list appears, select your printer. If you don't see your printer in the list, tap *All Printers* and search for it. If you do not know the name of your printer, refer to the printer's user manual.

7.) Select the quantity of copies you would like to print

8.) Tap *Print*

How to Set up and Access E-mail

To set up e-mail, go to the *APPS* tab at the top of the homepage (main screen). From there, locate the *E-mail* tab and tap on it.

There should now be a list of different *E-mail* types, such as *G-MAIL, YAHOO,* etc. Select the one you would like to use.

On the next screen, type in your e-mail address and enter the password. Then select the *Next* tab. It might also ask you for a description, as a reminder.

Next, you will be asked to type in the name that you would like to be addressed by when dealing with e-mail. This is the name that will be displayed when outgoing messages are sent by you.

You can also type in a nickname.

You may or may not see something that reads: *Send e-mail from this account by default* and *Import Contacts.*

Send e-mail from this account by default means that it will automatically send e-mail messages from that address. If you have multiple e-mail accounts and you would like to send different messages through different e-mail addresses, you might not want to have this box checked.

Import Contacts will place all of your contacts into the *Kindle* device automatically. If you are okay with that, make sure the box next to *Import Contacts* is checked.

Next, tap *View Your Inbox.*

The e-mail account should now be set up.

To set up another account, tap the square-shaped menu button at the bottom of the screen. From there, select the *accounts* tab.

Press the square-shaped menu button. Then tap the *Add Account* icon.

From there, repeat the same process as before.

When you'd like to access your e-mail account, go to the *APPS* tab, select *e-mail*, and go to *view inbox.*

Camera and Photos

The following chapters will deal with pictures, including how to take photos, how to transfer them to a computer, and how to share them.

How to Take Pictures

Go to the homepage (main screen) and tap **Photos** on the screen. Open the camera by tapping the **Camera** icon at the top-right portion of the screen.

To take a picture, tap the **shutter** button on the screen.

(Note.)When you are in camera mode, unless you swipe or tap on the screen to make the other buttons appear, there should only be one visible button on the screen.

After taking a picture, it should appear as a thumbnail at the bottom of the screen. To expand the picture, tap the thumbnail. If you have multiple pictures, you can scroll through them by swiping the screen from right to left and left to right.

If the pictures are coming out blurry, check to make sure the camera lens is clean. You can also try adjusting the camera settings.

While the photos are expanded, tap the screen to reveal more buttons. To the right, there should be a series of buttons.

The **envelope** icon allows you to attach the picture to an e-mail account.

The **trashcan** icon allows you to delete the picture. Once moved to the **trash** folder, you will have the option to restore them or permanently remove them. The items will be permanently removed automatically after being in the **trash** folder for thirty days.

The **pencil** icon will open a variety of editing features. From there, you can change the lighting, color, and tone of the picture.

To get back to the main photo screen, tap the **arrow** icon (back button).

Transferring Pictures to a Computer

Photos can be transferred to your *kindle* device through a USB cord. This will help free up space on your *kindle* device.

Using a USB cord, hook the computer up to the *kindle* device. The USB port should be on the bottom of the *kindle* tablet.

A small popup should appear on the computer, telling you what to do. But if not, go to *Computer* and look under *Portable Devices*. A *kindle* folder should show up on the screen. Double-click on the folder to open it. The pictures should be inside. Highlight the pictures and click *Import*.

To prevent data corruption, wait until your computer tells you it is safe to do so. There should be a popup that reads: *Safe To Remove Hardware*.

If you do not see the *Safe To Remove Hardware* popup, locate the USB icon at the bottom-right corner of the computer. Right-click the icon, and then left-click *Eject Kindle Fire*.

After this is complete, tap *Disconnect on* your *kindle* device.

Sharing Pictures

T o share pictures:

1.) Go to the homepage (main screen).

2.) Tap **photos**.

3.) Tap the **cloud** or **device** tab

4.) Tap the **share** icon.

There should be a list of icons consisting of **email**, **FACEBOOK**, etc.

5.) Tap the icon in which you would like to share your photos.

Using a Micro-SD Card

B ooks, music, and videos can be downloaded onto the Micro-SD card. Additionally, Photos and personal videos can be stored on the card, as well.

Inserting Micro-SD Card:

1.) Locate the Micro-SD slot. It is on the upper right side of the tablet.

2.) Open the hatch.

3.) Insert the card until it locks into place.

As long as the card is inserted, any supported content you download will automatically be stored on it. However, you can manage the type of content that gets stored on the card by adjusting your preferences.

To manage your SD card storage preferences:

1.) Using a downward motion, swipe the top of the screen.

2.) Tap *Settings.*

3.) Tap *Storage.*

4.) Look under *SD Card* and adjust the switch to turn Micro-SD card support *on* or *off.*

How to Use ALEXA

ALEXA is a voice-controlled service that gives you the option to have quick access to the information and entertainment you seek.

By pressing and asking, you can set alarms, set timers, check your calendar, switch on lights, switch on thermostats, turn on fans, get news, and more.

If you are using the ALEXA feature for the first time, make sure it is powered on.

To check to see if it is enabled:

1.) Use a downward motion to swipe at the top of the screen.

2.) Go to *Settings.*

3.) Tap *ALEXA.*

4.) Make sure the switch is set to the *on* position.

To activate ALEXA:

1.) Press and hold the *Home* button on your device.

2.) When the blue line emerges, ALEXA is good to go.

There is no need to address it as, "ALEXA." Simply give it a command or ask a question.

If any popups are displayed by ALEXA, you can dismiss them by tapping the *back* button.

By default, ALEXA is disabled with child profiles and secondary adult profiles, and it can not be switched on.

How to Enable Skills

Skills are voice-controlled capabilities that improve the *ALEXA* device's functionality. To illustrate, if you'd like *ALEXA* to tell you about specific upcoming events in your city, you would need to enable a specific skill for that.

Oftentimes, if you know the specific name of the skill you'd like to use, you can simply say, "*ALEXA*, enable [skill name]."

But sometimes certain skills need to be enabled through the *Amazon* website or the *ALEXA* app, while others might need to be activated by following the prompts from *ALEXA*.

Enable *Skills*

1.) Open the *ALEXA* app.

2.) Go to the menu and select **Skills**.

You can also go to the *Amazon* website and go into the *skills* section.

3.) Use the *search bar* to find a specific skill or browse through the skills by category.

4.) After finding the skill you'd like to use, select it to go to its detail page. The detail page should include at least one example of what to say to play or open the skill.

5.) On the skill's detail page, select **Enable Skill**.

Now you should be able to tell *ALEXA* to open the skill.

If you need help with the skill, say, "ALEXA, [skill name] help."

Manage *Skills*

1.) Open the *ALEXA* app.

2.) Go to the menu and select **Skills**.

3.) Select **Your Skills**.

4.) Select a *skill* to go to its detail page.

You should now see a list of available options.

Asking ALEXA a Question

You can ask *ALEXA* questions about people, simple calculations, dates, weather, traffic, sports, and more.

To illustrate:

- *"What's the weather?"* (You will need to program your location into the *ALEXA* app before you can ask it what the weather is like in your town.)

- *"How's traffic?"*

- *"How many liters are in a gallon?"*

- *"What's the score of the [team] game?"*

- "How do you spell [word]?"

- "What is the definition of [word]?"

Giving ALEXA Commands

You can set alarms, timers, and reminders with ALEXA.

To create a reminder or edit an existing one:

1.) Go to the menu.

2.) Select *Reminders & Alarms.*

3.) At the top of the screen, there should be a drop-down menu. Select your device.

4.) Select the *Reminders* tab.

5.) If you'd like to create a new reminder, select *+Add Reminder.* If you'd like to manage a reminder, select the reminder you want to manage, then select *Edit Reminder* or *Mark as Completed*

If you'd like to set a reminder, say, *"Remind me to [task]."*

ALEXA will tell you the reminder when it is time for the scheduled task to take place.

Timers can also be used. For example, if you have something cooking on the stove, you might want to multitask by doing something else in the meantime. Using a timer can help you multitask without allowing the food to overcook.

You can name your timers and set time duration. Speak to the advice and tell it what you would like it to do.

To illustrate:

- "Set a stove timer for thirty minutes."

- "Set a laundry timer for twenty minutes."

You can also cancel a timer by saying, "Cancel the timer."

Or you can ask, "How much time is left on my timer?"

If you'd like to **manage a timer**:

1.) Open the ALEXA app.

2.) Look at the menu and select *Reminders & Alarms.*

3.) Select your device from the drop-down menu.

4.) Select *Timers.*

5.) Go to the timer you'd like to manage.

6.) Select *Pause* or *Cancel.*

To set an alarm, say, "Set an alarm for [time]."

To manage alarms:

1.) Open the *ALEXA* app.

2.) Go to the *Menu.*

2.) Select *Timers & Alarms.*

3.) Select your device from the drop-down menu.

4.) Choose *Alarms.*

5.) Select the alarm you'd like to manage.

6.) Look under *Repeats* and choose an option.

7.) When finished, select *Save Changes.*

ALEXA Command and Request List

Basics

"Turn up the volume."

"Turn down the volume."

"Let's chat."

"Stop."

"Go to sleep."

"Help."

Music

"Next song."

"Skip song."

"Previous song."

"Pause in [room name]."

"Resume in [room name]."

"Play the next track in [room name]."

"Louder in [room name]."

"Quieter in [room name]."

"Set the volume to [volume number or percentage] in [room name]."

"Mute [room name]."

"Turn it up in [room name]."

"What's playing in [room name]?"

"Play music by [artist]."

"What's this song?"

"Buy [album name] by [artist's name]."

"Play the top songs this week."

"Play my [playlist name] playlist."

"Shuffle my new music."

"Shop for new music by [artist's name]."

"Play the [station name] on [music service name]."

"Add this song."

"Who sings the song [song title]?"

"Who is in the band [band's name]?"

"Sample songs by [artist]."

To-do lists

"Add [item] to my shopping list."

"Create a to-do list."

"Put [task] on my to-do list."

"I need to [task]."

Shopping on *Amazon*

Note: To place orders with ALEXA, certain requirements must first be met, including being an *Amazon Prime* member.

In summary, you will need:

An annual or 30-day free trial *Amazon Prime* membership.

A U.S. shipping address.

Voice purchasing enabled in the *ALEXA* app.

A payment method issued by a U.S. bank with a U.S. billing address set up in your 1-Click settings.

A device with access to the *ALEXA Voice Service*.

"Add [item] to my cart."

"Buy [product]."

"Order [item]."

"Reorder [item]."

"Where's my stuff?"

"Track my order."

Smart Home

Note: To find compatible *smart home* devices, simply search for *amazon ALEXA supported smart home devices*.

"Discover my *smart home* devices."

"BLUETOOTH."

"Connect to my phone."

"Is the front / back door locked?"

"Lock the front / back door."

"Turn on the lights."

"Turn on the TV."

"Raise the temperature [number] degrees."

"Set the temperature to [number]."

"What's the temperature in here?"

"What's the thermostat set to?"

"Make the living room [color]."

"Turn the desk lamp to [color]."

"Turn on the hallway light."

"Turn on *Movie Time*."

"Dim the living room to [percentage]."

"Set the fan to [percentage]."

Weather

Note: To obtain your weather forecast, you will need to add your address to the *ALEXA* app.

"What's the weather in [name of city]."

"What's the temperature?"

"What will the weather be like in [name of city] tomorrow?"

"What's the extended forecast for [name of city]."

"Is it going to rain today?"

"Will it snow tomorrow?"

"Will I need an umbrella today?"

Traffic and Local Information

Note: To get local information, you will need to add your address to the *ALEXA* app. To check traffic, you will first need to set your starting and destination points in the *ALEXA* app.

"How is traffic?"

"What's my commute like?"

"What are the business hours of [venue name]?"

"What [venues] are nearby?"

"What time is the movie, [film name] playing?"

"Find the address for [place]."

"Is [venue] open?"

"Ask *UBER* to request a ride."

News

"What's in the news?"

"Give me my flash briefing."

"Open [publication name]."

"Pause."

"Next."

"Previous."

Sports

"Give me my sports update."

"What was the score of the [name of team] game?"

"Did the [team's name] win?"

"When do the [team's name] play next?"

Alarm Clock

"Set an alarm for [time]."

"When's my next alarm?"

"Snooze."

"Set a timer for [time length]."

"Set a second timer for [time]."

"Cancel my alarm for [time]."

"What time is it?"

"Cancel all alarms."

"Set a repeating alarm for [time] [days]."

Calendar

"What's the date?"

"Add an event to my calendar."

"Add a [time and event] to my calendar.

"What's on my calendar today?"

"What's my next appointment?"

Knowledge

"How tall is [name of mountain]?"

"How deep is [name of ocean]?"

"What's the capital of [place]?"

"What's the population of [place]?"

"Who wrote [name of book]?"

"What's the definition of [word]?"

"How do you spell [word]?"

"What's [number] times [number]?"

"[Number] factorial?"

AUDIOBOOKS

"Play [book title] on *Audible*."

"Pause."

"Resume."

"Next chapter."

"Previous chapter."

"Go to last chapter."

"Go to [chapter number]."

Just for Fun

"Tell me a joke."

"Sing a song."

"Tell me a story."

"Play a game."

<u>How to Connect *Smart* Home Devices to *ALEXA*</u>

B̲efore connecting a *smart home* device to *ALEXA*, it's important to be familiar with the safety information.

<u>Safety Guidelines</u>

• Follow the instructions for *smart home* devices.

• After a request is made, confirm the action has been completed on the *smart home* device.

• Make sure your *ALEXA* supported device and connected products are running efficiently. For example, make sure the *lock doors* feature is working before you leave your home.

<u>How to Connect a *Smart Home* Device to *ALEXA* in The *ALEXA* App</u>

1.) Go to the menu and select **Skills**.

2.) Search for and locate the skill you are looking for, then select **Enable**.

3.) Follow the on-screen directions to get through the linking process.

4.) Tell *ALEXA* to discover the device by saying "Discover my devices." You can also go into the **Smart Home** section in the *ALEXA* app and select **Add Device**.

<u>How to Discover *Smart Home* Devices without a skill</u>

Not all devices require a skill to connect to *ALEXA*.

If you'd like to connect these devices, simply tell *ALEXA* to "Discover devices."

Some devices might need to be powered on before they can be discovered. For example, if you are using a *Phillips Hue Bridge*, press the button on the bridge before attempting to discover the device.

How to Manage Connected *Smart Home* Devices

I t is possible to edit a device's name, disable a device, or delete a device.

1.) Go to the menu in the *ALEXA* app.

2.) Tap **Smart Home**.

3.) Select **Devices**.

4.) Select you *smart home* device.

5.) Select **Edit**.

If you'd like to disable all devices associated to a specific skill, rather than delete the devices one at a time, you can simply disable the skill.

Say, "Disable [skill's name] skill."

You can also:

1.) Go to the menu in the *ALEXA* app

2.) Select **Skills**

3.) Select **Your Skills**

4.) Select a skill.

5.) You should now see a *skill* detail page. Select the *Disable* tab.

How to Enable and Customize Voice-View Screen Reader

T he *Voice-View Screen Reader* reads out loud the items you touch on the screen. It will also describe the actions you make on screen.

Enable *Voice-View Screen Reader*

1.) Press and hold the power button until you hear an alert.

2.) Hold two fingers (slightly apart) on the screen for approximately five seconds.

Customize *Voice-View Screen Reader*

Customizing the settings will allow you to adjust reading speed, speech volume, sounds volume, punctuation level, and more.

1.) When *Voice-View* is on, use three fingers to swipe downward from the top portion of the screen.

2.) Focus on **Settings**, then double-tap to activate.

To go to **Accessibility**, double-tap to activate.

Gestures

Stop speech: Single-tap with two fingers.

Start or stop dictation: Double-tap with two fingers wile editing text.

Start or stop media: Double-tap with two fingers.

Read all from selected item: Swipe downward with two fingers.

Read all from first item: Swipe upward with two fingers.

Make an *ALEXA* request: Double-tap and hold with two fingers.

Turn screen curtain on or off: Triple-tap with three fingers.

Go to the first item on screen: Tap on upper portion of screen with 4 fingers.

Go to the last item on screen: Tap on lower portion of screen with four fingers.

Turn speech on or off: Double-tap with three fingers.

Enter or exit *Learn Mode* for gesture practice: Double-tap with 4 fingers.

How to Read Books with *Voice-View*

When *Voice-View* is enabled, you can use gestures and Text-to-Speech to read and interact with a book.

You can choose between *continuous reading* mode (reads all the pages of the book) and *non-continuous reading* mode (reads a page, character, or word on the page).

Begin Reading

From the book, swipe downward from the upper portion of the page with two fingers when the reading toolbar is closed to begin reading from the top of the page. To begin reading from the current focus point, use an L gesture.

When a book is opened, Text-to-Speech starts reading and will automatically turn the pages.

Switch from *Continuous Reading* mode to *Non-Continuous reading* mode

Tap the screen

Make the adjustment

Show reading toolbar

While reading, tap the screen once, then double-tap.

Adjust *Continuous Reading* speed

When the reading toolbar is open, the control for *Continuous Reading* speed will be at the bottom-right corner of the screen.

Tap the control, then double-tap the screen.

Change Reading Voice

1.) Make sure the reading bar is open.

2.) Use two fingers to swipe downward from the upper portion of the screen to open **Quick Actions**.

3.) Select **Settings**.

4.) Select **Keyboard & Language**

5.) Select **Text-to-Speech**.

Read one page, paragraph, word, or character at a time

1.) Using a continuous motion, swipe upward then to the right with one finger to activate the **Local Context Menu**.

2.) Select your preferred reading level.

Turn page

◆To go to the next page, swipe left with two fingers. To go to the previous page, swipe right with two fingers.

Read additional content

1.) Double-tap a selection when highlights, footnotes, alternate text, and Word Wise are announced.

2.) Swipe left or right to read the text before or after selected content.

Open the Go To Menu

1.) Swipe from the left portion of the screen with two fingers.

2.) Double-tap a chapter or section.

Select Text

1.) Maneuver across the screen with one finger to locate the word you'd like to select.

2.) Double-tap the word, then hold to listen to its definition.

Note: It is also possible to swipe to the left or right to choose a highlight color, add a note, share notes and highlights, and more.

Adjust Text Selection

1.) Go to the menu and select the markers to increase or decrease the text size. The selection markers should be available in the menu after selecting a text size.

<u>How to Enable and Use *Screen Magnifier*</u>

T he *Screen Magnifier* allows you to enlarge items on the screen.

1.) Swipe downward from the top of the screen and go to **Settings**.

2.) Select **Accessibility**.

3.) Select **Screen Magnifier**.

Once enabled, *Screen Magnifier* can magnify the screen and adjust the zoom level.

Here's how it works:

Magnify the screen: Triple-tap the screen with one finger.

Temporarily magnify the screen: Triple-tap the screen with one finger and hold it on the screen. To pan, drag your finger around the screen.

Pan: Drag two fingers (slightly apart) across the screen.

Change zoom level: When the screen is magnified, pinch inward or outward with two fingers.

Maintenance

Maintaining your *Kindle* device at regular intervals will keep it running more efficiently.

Keep your tablet out of water (rain, spills, etc). If the tablet does become wet, turn off the wireless feature and unplug the cables. Dry the device with a nonabrasive cloth. Wait until the device is entirely dry before powering it back on.

If you choose to put the tablet in a backpack or suitcase, either use a cover or keep it cushioned between nonabrasive fabric to prevent scratches.

Do not bring or leave your *Kindle* device in extreme weather conditions. Keep it out of excessive heat and freezing conditions.

Unless you are certain you know what you are doing, replacing the battery on the *Kindle Fire HD 10* should only be done by a professional service provider.

When bringing the device onto an aircraft, make sure you follow all rules and regulations. Using electronic devices on airplanes can interfere with their systems.

Troubleshooting

As with most electronic devices, the *Fire HD* tablet is prone to occasional glitches. Many of these glitches can usually be solved by simply restarting the device.

To restart the device:

1.) Press and hold the power button for a few moments.

2.) When the prompt appears, tap *Shut Down.*

3.) Wait for the tablet to shut down.

4.) Press the power button to power the device back on.

If the screen is entirely frozen, a forced reset can be performed.

To **perform a forced reset:**

1.) Press and hold the power button for ten to twenty seconds or until the *Kindle Fire* restarts automatically.

2.) Wait for the screen to go black. This usually means the tablet is off.

3.) Power the device back on.

But the glitches are not always that simple to remedy, and additional steps may be required.

Here are some glitches and how to fix them:

Tablet will not turn on

• Make sure your *Kindle Fire* is charged.

• Make sure the battery is not dead. To check, connect the device to the charger. If there is no sign that the battery is charging, the battery or charger may need to be replaced. To determine if it's a charger issue, try using a separate charger and see if the result remains the same.

Screen is not responding to tapping or other commands

• Make sure the battery is not running low.

• Verify that the screen is not just temporarily frozen. To verify, wait twenty minutes or so for the screen to begin functioning again. If it remains unresponsive, try restarting the tablet.

• Inspect the screen for visible damage (stains, marks, large abrasions, etc.)

Audio through headphones is low quality

• Verify that the cord for the headphones is fully (not just partially) plugged into the jack.

• Try using a different pair of headphones.

<u>Unable to Purchase or Access Content</u>

• Verify that the *Kindle Fire* is connected to the Internet.

• If using WI-FI, try turning the WI-FI feature off and back on.

• Go to a different area and see if the WI-FI signal improves.

How to Fix WI-FI Connectivity Issues

Connectivity issues can be caused by a variety of things, and oftentimes, the problem can be rectified by simply restarting the router. The router can be restarted by unplugging it (powering it off) and then plugging it back in (powering it on).

But sometimes it's not that easy, so here are some other things that can be tried.

• If you are getting an error that says, *content could not be downloaded because of a network connectivity error*, start by going to *settings*. Go to *More.* Then scroll down to where it says, *date and time*. Set it to *automatic*. Internet problems can be caused by incorrect date and time.

For all other internet connectivity problems, try the following ideas:

• In the *Wireless* menu, make sure the WI-FI connection is turn on.

• If you are trying to connect to a network and it says, *authentication failed*, tap on the network icon and click the *Forget* icon. Then reopen it and try again. If it still fails to connect, try unplugging the router or modem. Then plug it back in, wait several minutes for it to reboot, and try to connect again.

• Check the router settings and make sure that the router is not set to the wrong channel. Make sure the router is set to use a channel from 1 to 11.

• Using a downward motion, swipe the top of the screen. An icon titled, *Wireless* should emerge. Click on it and make sure *Airplane Mode* is turned off.

• Using a downward motion, swipe the top of the screen. Tap the *Help* icon. Then tap the *Device Health* icon. See if your device is alerting you of any problems.

• Make sure your device is running the latest software version. Sometimes installing an update can fix the problem. But since you are unable to connect to the internet, you will have to download the update through a computer that is able to connect to the web. This can be accomplished by connecting the tablet to the computer through the use of a USB cord.

• If you can't locate your network, it might be hidden. To check, tap the *Add Network* icon. From there, type in the name of the network. After typing in the name, type in the password and see if you are able to connect.

If a connection is still unable to be established, you may have to refer to your ISP (Internet Service Provider).